HAVANA

THE CITY AT A GLANCE

Castillo del Morro
Built in 1630 to defend the city, it has an embarrassing track record, and the views of Habana Vieja from the restaurant Los XII Apóstoles (see p062) are superb.
Carretera de la Cabaña, T 863 7063

Hotel Nacional de Cuba
McKim, Mead and White's architectural double kiss perches on a cliff above the Straits of Florida. Its bunker network assumed strategic importance during the Cuban Missile Crisis.
See p017

Malecón
This porticoed seafront promenade, which has been ravaged by hurricanes and corroded by salt, is the epicentre of Havana social life.

Habana Vieja
The city was founded here in 1519 and the old town's unique mélange of colonial architecture was declared a World Heritage Site in 1982.

Hermanos Ameijeiras Hospital
Conceived as a bank in the 1950s, this tower was converted into a hospital post-revolution, but still houses the national vault in its bowels.
See p012

Capitolio Nacional
The Americans left an indelible mark in 1928 with the monumental, neoclassical Capitolio. Its interiors drip with marble and gold leaf.
Calle Industria y Barcelona, T 863 7861

Compañía Cubana de Teléfonos
This terracotta-iced wedding cake was built for the Cuban Telephone Company in 1927. Leonardo Morales' whimsical neoclassicism would later shape swathes of El Vedado.
Aguila 565 esq Dragones

INTRODUCTION
THE CHANGING FACE OF THE URBAN SCENE

Havana today is like one of its blushing *quinceañeras*, a teenage girl on the verge of womanhood and freedom from an overbearing father. When released from the Castro legacy, what will Havana's citizens decide to make of their lives, of this glorious opportunity? How will they plan for the city's future if, indeed, anyone stays at home long enough to do so? Will the Miami relatives fly back to assume guardianship, lugging crates of Coca-Cola and clutching McDonald's blueprints, or will they decide that, actually, they're quite happy where they are, thank you very much?

The architectural attraction of Havana is that it is virgin territory. With no money or resources, nothing has been bulldozed to make way for something 'better'. It is an urban planning open textbook, a living demonstration of how a conurbation grows, each of its districts distinguished by outstanding examples of the *en vogue* styles of the era. The worry is that this innocent city will be seduced and corrupted by the blue eyes and the greenbacks. Efforts are being made to preserve its integrity – the colonial core is currently being restored – but other areas are in dire need of a protection order.

Yet perhaps the most astonishing thing about Havana is the *joie de vivre* of its citizens. Habaneros have learnt that good things come to those who wait, and so they might as well face the music and dance in the meantime. Nothing major will change here for at least five years, but now is the time to go – before it does.

ESSENTIAL INFO

FACTS, FIGURES AND USEFUL ADDRESSES

TOURIST OFFICE
Infotur
Calle Obispo y San Ignacio
T 636 884
www.infotur.cu

TRANSPORT
Car hire
Transtur
T 553 991
www.transtur.cu
Havanautos
T 203 9658
www.havanautos.cu
Taxis
Panataxi
T 555 555
Micar
T 204 2444
Taxi OK
T 877 6666

EMERGENCY SERVICES
Ambulance
T 405 093
Police
T 820 106
24-hour pharmacy
Clinica Central Cira Garcia
Calle 20, 4101 esq 41
T 204 2811
www.cirag.cu

CONSULATES
British Consulate
Calle 34, 702-704 esq 7ma
T 204 1771
www.britishembassy.gov.uk
US Interests Section of Swiss Embassy
Calle Calzada entre L y M
T 833 3551
havana.usinterestsection.gov

MONEY
Asistur
Paseo Martí 208
T 866 8339
www.asistur.cu

POSTAL SERVICES
Post Office
Hotel Nacional de Cuba
Calle 21 y O
T 836 3564
Shipping
DHL
Avenida 1ra y 26
T 204 1876
www.dhl.com

BOOKS
Cuba and the Night by Pico Iyer (Vintage)
Revolution of Forms: Cuba's Forgotten Art Schools by John A Loomis (Princeton Architectural Press)

WEBSITES
Art/Design
www.cubanow.net
www.cubarte-english.cult.cu
Newspaper
www.periodico26.cu

COST OF LIVING
Taxi from José Martí Airport to city centre
€19
Coffee
€0.50
Packet of cigarettes
€2.25
Daily newspaper
Free
Bottle of champagne
€150

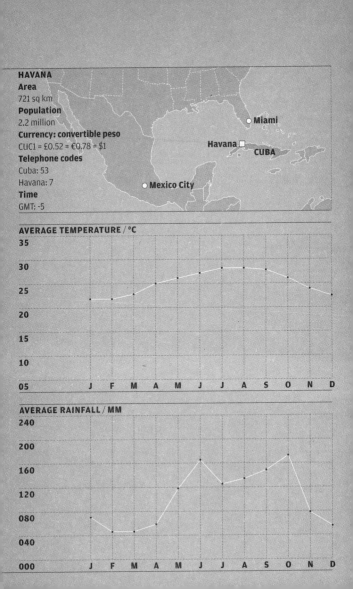

HAVANA
Area
721 sq km
Population
2.2 million
Currency: convertible peso
CUC1 = £0.52 = €0.78 = $1
Telephone codes
Cuba: 53
Havana: 7
Time
GMT: -5

Miami

Havana ☐ CUBA

● Mexico City

AVERAGE TEMPERATURE / °C

35												
30												
25												
20												
15												
10												
05	J	F	M	A	M	J	J	A	S	O	N	D

AVERAGE RAINFALL / MM

240												
200												
160												
120												
080												
040												
000	J	F	M	A	M	J	J	A	S	O	N	D

NEIGHBOURHOODS

THE AREAS YOU NEED TO KNOW AND WHY

To help you navigate the city, we've chosen the most interesting districts (see the map inside the back cover) and underlined featured venues in colour, according to their location (see below); those venues that are outside these areas are not coloured.

PLAZA DE LA REVOLUCIÓN

This monumental expanse, built to impress in 1958 by Batista, was soon commandeered by Castro for the same purpose. The square is surrounded by government ministries, the Teatro Nacional (see p068) and the obelisk memorial to José Martí, as much a revolutionary hero as the two Cs. Among all this puffed-out-chest architecture are sweet touches of everyday life, such as the musicians practising among the trees.

MIRAMAR

This district was settled in the 1940s as the rich moved west from El Vedado to build ostentatious mansions and private clubs, which Castro reappropriated as public buildings and embassies. Here are some of the few new builds – Antonio Quintana's 1979 Palacio de las Convenciones (Avenida 146) and José Antonio Choy's 1997 Banco Financiero Internacional remodel (Avenida 5ta, 9009 y 92) – plus fancy restaurants for all the businessmen and diplomats.

HABANA VIEJA

The architecture of the old town is a superb mix of baroque, Moorish, colonial and art nouveau flourish that is currently under restoration. Obispo is a riot of restaurants, bars, shops, hustlers and live salsa in the afternoon/early evening, but wander a few streets off this main drag where crumbling façades are kept up by improvised wooden beams, and you will find it a lot harder to buy a dodgy box of banana-leaf cigars.

LA RAMPA

The heart of the casino and gambling halls of the 1950s, the steep incline of La Rampa is still a popular strut for Habaneros of all ages and is lined with bars, cafés, cinemas, matinee clubs and salsa dives, stretching from the Hotel Nacional (see p017) up to the city's modernist core and Saturday-night date venues of choice: Cine Yara (see p074), Coppelia (see p036) ice-cream parlour and hotel Habana Libre (see p026).

EL VEDADO

It was here that Havana high society spread in the first half of the 20th century. The cultured El Vedado boasts theatres, parks and museums, such as the Museo de Artes Decorativos (Calle 17, 502, T 830 9848), and a gamut of architectural styles. Among the neoclassical and Italianate villas are the brutalist Edificio Girón (Malecón entre E y F), the 1950s modernism of Hotel Riviera (see p030) and the art deco Casa de las Américas (Calle G y 3ta, T 552 706).

PARQUE CENTRAL

The closest Cuba gets to Piccadilly Circus (ie, look before you cross the road), this square is surrounded by hotels and public buildings, such as Paul Belau's ornate 1915 Gran Teatro (Paseo Martí 458, T 861 3077). It's bordered by Chinatown's faded dragon and the war zone of Centro, while grand old Paseo shuffles down to the Malecón. Watch the action from the veranda bar of Hotel Inglaterra (Paseo Martí 416, T 860 8595).

LANDMARKS

THE SHAPE OF THE CITY SKYLINE

The best way to get a handle on Havana is to ride the painfully slow elevators of the 137m José Martí Memorial (Calle Paseo y Avenida Independencia) or the 123m Edificio FOCSA (see p010). From either of these two lookouts, you can see a city virtually unchanged since the 1959 revolution. There are no gleaming skyscrapers of other world metropolises, but at least the few high rises that do exist stand out as reference points in the flat Havana skyline.

The main districts can be identified by a single building, which is useful as asking a Cuban for directions is generally fruitless. The incongruous Capitolio Nacional (Calle Industria y Barcelona, T 860 3411), a copycat of the Capitol in Washington DC, dominates Parque Central and Habana Vieja; the Hotel Nacional de Cuba (see p017) is the lynchpin of La Rampa; the modernist Hotel Riviera (see p030) signals the Vedado seafront; and across the Rio Almendares, the Russian Embassy (see p013) is the unloved beacon of west Miramar. One more useful anchor is the hub of Plaza de la Revolución, from which wide boulevards lead to all corners of the city.

But Havana is not so much about its crumbling architecture, but its inhabitants and how they manage to cope with it. Nowhere is that more apparent than along the Malecón (see p038), the seafront promenade that commands the north of the city, where every aspect of Cuban life takes place from dusk over countless bottles of rum. *For full addresses, see Resources.*

Edificio FOCSA
Cuba's tallest residential structure went up in 1956. Built in concrete in a flat Y shape by Ernesto Gómez-Sampera and Martin Domínguez as luxury flats, the Corbusian-style complex included shops, offices, a school and a cinema, many of which are now in disrepair. However, the renovated top-floor French restaurant La Torre (T 553 088) has stunning views.
Calle 17 entre M y N

Hermanos Ameijeiras Hospital

As the only structure above three storeys in Centro, the largest hospital in Cuba sticks out like a sore thumb. Its modernist, yellowy concrete, 23-storey winged tower and expansive plaza scream high finance, and it is a fine example of a construction started under Batista (it was intended to be the National Bank of Cuba) that was converted post-revolution to provide a more socialist function. Standing on an imposing concrete platform overlooking the Malecón, the building was reconfigured internally for its present use and has the best medical facilities on the island. But that's not saying too much, as decades of ill-conceived embargos have meant that medicines are extremely scarce. So you'd be best advised to look after your health and admire the building from the outside. *San Lázaro y Belascoaín*

Russian Embassy

The locals will tell you it's ugly, but the 20-storey tower of the Russian Embassy is a striking, if sinister, example of 1980s Soviet architecture. This concrete and glass complex in Miramar stands among the mansions of the nouveaux riches that were converted into consulates and offices after the revolution. Like a one-fingered salute to the sky and to the USA, it evokes memories of the space race. Once home to hundreds of Moscow diplomats, since the break-up of the USSR, all that's left of their legacy is the stretch Ladas that bounce around the city's potholes. Now a skeleton staff rattles around the marble salons and windowless rooms, many of which have been permanently closed. The building stands, like so much of Havana, as a sad symbol of Cuba's lost history.

Avenida 5ta, 6402 entre 62 y 66

Ministry of the Interior

This government building designed by
Aquiles Capablanca in 1953 is the most
accomplished in Plaza de la Revolución.
Clad in stone from Jaimanitas like many
of the other government buildings in the
square, offices are shielded from the sun
by brises-soleils, and a ceramic mural by
Amelia Peláez adorns the entrance, but
the building only achieved its tourist-trap
status in the late 1960s with the addition
to the concave elevator block of the 30m
blackened steel frieze of former Minister
of the Interior Che Guevara. Based on the
iconic photo taken by Alberto Korda in
1960, it carries the revolutionary slogan
Hasta la Victoria Siempre (Forever Onwards
Towards Victory) and even lights up at
night. Erected as a backdrop to a memorial
address that was given by Castro after
Guevara was killed in Bolivia in 1967, the
sculpture has remained here ever since.
Plaza de la Revolución

HOTELS

WHERE TO STAY AND WHICH ROOMS TO BOOK

When choosing a pad, consider location, architecture and whether or not you want a pool. Public spaces are stunning at the classic hotels, such as the Nacional (opposite) and the Riviera (see p030), but rooms are unloved. Cuba has embraced tourism as its only cash cow, yet is investing purely in Habana Vieja, where 18 dilapidated colonial buildings have been turned into boutiquey, themed hotels run by staff who, unusually for state-run establishments, don't look as if they'd rather pull teeth. Try Santa Isabel (Baratillo 9, T 860 8201), in an 18th-century palace, or the art nouveau Palacio Cueto (Inquisidor 351), due to reopen in 2007. There is a raft of decent hotels in El Vedado, many built during the 1950s casino boom, but leave the Miramar resorts in their seafront carpark wasteland.

Private accommodation in *casas particulares* is at a zenith since Castro legalised it in the 1990s. Forget the authenticity of a room in a family home – hire a private villa, often for the same price as a hotel room (although a maid and chauffeur are extra), such as the six-bed La Mansion (T 205 7959, www.rentincuba.com) or seafront Casa Raul (Calle 15, 153, T 290 1491), complete with pool.

Just don't come here expecting wi-fi and goosedown – hotel publicity boasts of clothes hangers in bathrooms and alarm-clock radios. Be wary of beds, worn out from overuse, Cuban-style. And remember, you're lucky to get hot water – everything else is a bonus. *For full addresses and room rates, see Resources.*

Hotel Nacional de Cuba

The most famous hotel in Cuba has hosted Churchill and Sinatra and flown the flag for Cuban hospitality since 1930. McKim, Mead and White's conflation of art deco, neoclassical and neocolonial uses Cuban marble, Jaimanita stone and clay tiles. Interiors impress from the moment you enter the lobby (above), with its Sevillan mosaics, hardwood ceilings, chandeliers, antiques and original iron-grille elevators.

However, the Nacional's 426-room bulk has failed to budge with the times, and it is now overrun with tourist groups. At least that means the food is of a high quality, notably in restaurant Comedor de Aguiar, as long as Michael Keaton's face on the menu doesn't put you off. Have a nosey around and a daiquiri under the garden cloisters.
Calle O esq 21, T 836 3564,
www.hotelnacionaldecuba.com

Hotel Nacional de Cuba

Meliá Cohiba
Typical of the vast complexes built by joint ventures in the 1990s, the Cohiba is a frosty behemoth, but if you're here on business, amenities are faultless. Its concertina façade toys with perspective, with graphic lines and tinted windows, but character is only provided by the pool and the Expresso Bar (pictured).
Avenida Paseo entre 1ra y 3ra, T 833 3636, www.solmeliacuba.com

Hotel Florida

Florida is in the thick of the Habana Vieja mêlée, but wander inside its two-tiered, porticoed atrium (above), settle into a wicker chair among the foliage and calm descends. This 1836 former noble family residence is imposing, yet the hotel itself retains an elegant intimacy. There are 25 spacious, colonial-style rooms, with wrought-iron beds and furnishings, high-beamed ceilings, blue and white porcelain, and diamond-checked Italian marble floors, a feature throughout the hotel. Request the corner Suite 18 on the second floor for louvred wooden shutters that open onto a large balcony. The Piano Bar Margato is popular for its live music and because it's one of the few places in Habana Vieja that stays open late. Have a nightcap under its stained-glass roof. *Calle Obispo 252 esq Cuba, T 862 4127*

Hotel Saratoga

It may not be the most architecturally exciting, but for luxury and convenience, Saratoga is hands down the best place to stay in town. Behind its neoclassical shell, this 1933 hotel was gutted and reopened in 2005 with reproduction features, such as 1930s furnishings, colourful floor tiles and a central atrium, combined with the latest technology, such as wi-fi in public areas, and contemporary elements, such as the mural by Juan Carlos Botello in the palm-fringed 24-hour Mezzanine Bar. The Saratoga rooms face the Capitolio, but for real indulgence, book the 100 sq m Habana Suite (overleaf), with its marble, mahogany and three balconies. Service is European standard and the pretty rooftop pool (above) has a 270-degree panorama. *Paseo Martí 603 esq Dragones, T 868 1000, www.hotel-saratoga.com*

Habana Suite, Hotel Saratoga

Tryp Habana Libre

Welton Becket and Associates' modernist landmark at the top of La Rampa towers 125m above street level. It made a strong statement of capitalist intent in 1958, but Castro turned the tables 10 months later, when he chose the Presidential Suite La Castellana as his HQ during the first days of the revolution; guests can ask reception for a tour. The Libre's still as relevant today; buzzy and hip with a Latino clientele. The best rooms are the highest, with recessed balconies overlooking the pool (left) and beyond. There's a take on Morris Lapidus in the lobby (above), with its skylighted dome, the top-floor club Turquino has a retractable roof for salsa under the stars, and Amelia Peláez's mural on the plinth has become a symbol of the entire city. *Calle L esq 23, T 834 6100, www.solmeliacuba.com*

Hotel Raquel

Upholding the city's esteemed lobby tradition, the Raquel has a magnificent stained-glass roof that invites the sun to flood in and warm its ornate, gilded marble columns and statuettes (right). A fine example of the restoration of Habana Vieja, the building in the old Jewish quarter was designed for a fabric-importing firm in 1908 by Venezuelan architect Naranjo Ferrer, and the marble staircase, iron elevator and art nouveau façade are original; the Old Testament theme is new. Restaurant Jardín del Edén is kosher, the only place in Cuba to find borscht and Hungarian goulash, and the 25 rooms have brass beds, turn-of-the-century furnishings and paintings by well-known Cuban artists. Ask for one of the three with a terrace, or opt for better views from a top-floor room with balcony. *Calle Amargura esq San Ignacio, T 860 8280, www.habaguanex.com*

Hotel Riviera

The Miami firm Polevitzky, Johnson and Associates excelled with the 1957 design of this green and grey seafront pleasure palace – a pre-revolution gambling mecca under mafia boss Meyer Lansky. The egg-shaped, ceramic-clad dome housed the former casino, now more likely to be used for bingo conventions, while underneath the hotel's elongated concrete tongue, the Copa Room cabaret and the low-ceilinged, low-furnished lobby (pictured), with its truncated staircase, abstract sculptures by Cuban Florencio Gelabert and wooden latticework, are both museum pieces. Shame the 352 tatty rooms don't match up. Come for a Martini in the lobby bar or a dive in the pool from the triple-tiered Christmas-tree board.
Paseo y Malecón, T 836 4051,
www.grancaribe.cu

24 HOURS

SEE THE BEST OF THE CITY IN JUST ONE DAY

There's many a soul who's spent an entire 24 hours in Havana partying – step forward Mr Hemingway – and abstinence is nigh on impossible in this city. But between the mojitos and the kicking, inescapable salsa, which both flow from dawn to dawn, take in the city's highlights as well as each district's unique architectural cachet. After brekkie and finding your bearings from the top of the Sevilla (opposite), stroll through Habana Vieja; half-ruined, half-restored. Cross cigars off your to-do list at Partagás (see p034) and art deco with a coffee in the Edificio Bacardí (see p065), before culture at the Museo de la Revolución (see p035) or the Cuban wing of the Museo de Bellas Artes (Calle Trocadero, T 861 3858) next door.

Hail a taxi to La Rampa, but don't count on your driver having the faintest idea where he's going – he's probably a civil engineer. Your 24 hours should include some queueing to be truly authentic, so wait in line at Coppelia (see p036), which scoops ice cream for 35,000 Habaneros a day, before an early evening gander along the Malecón, an architour all of its own. If La Guarida (see p039) is fully booked, the classy French restaurant La Torre (see p010) has incredible 360-degree views. Afterwards, Casa de la Música (see p060) puts on world-class salsa acts every night, provoking some outrageous dancing. And remember, if you enounter any problems, even a modest *propina* (tip) gets you an *extremely* long way. *For full addresses, see Resources.*

08.30 Roof Garden, Sevilla Hotel

Breakfast in the ninth-floor restaurant at the Sevilla, where there's a fine spread with buffet and menu options, such as eggs with rice, beans and *tostones* (fried plantain crisps). Architects Antonio and Rogelio Rodríguez's 1908 design for this hotel was inspired by Granada's Alhambra and the turn-of-the-century lobby is an impressive tribute of arcades, columns, mosaics and Mudéjar tiles, kept cool and airy by its whirring ceiling fans, while the eclectic façade is a mix of classical columns and neo-Moorish touches. Al Capone once stayed here – he booked the entire sixth floor for his entourage – but these days the rooms and pool look tired, so sleep elsewhere. After your fill, take a postprandial *paseo* around Habana Vieja. *Sofitel Sevilla Hotel, Calle Trocadero 55, T 860 8560, www.sofitel.com*

11.30 Real Fabrica de Tabacos Partagás

Even if you don't smoke, cigars, and more specifically the peddling of them, pervades every waking moment in Cuba, so you may as well see how they're made. The Partagás factory's façade, with its decorative high roof and iron balconies, is an impressive example of mid 19th-century colonial industrial architecture. Today the factory produces 12 million *puros* a year, most of which are rolled by hand, each worker specialising in a particular *vitola* (size). Brands such as Montecristo, Cohiba and Romeo y Julieta complement Partagás' range, which has an earthy, dense taste. A *lector* still reads the papers to the 700 employees but, sadly, cigars are not rolled on the thighs of virgins. Whether or not that was just an urban myth, or the city simply ran out of them, remains a mystery. *Calle Industria 520, T 862 4604*

13.00 Museo de la Revolución

You can't escape politics in this country, so get the Cuban perspective inside the 1920 Presidential Palace by Belgian Paul Belau and local Carlos Maruri, a riot of classical allusions and Spanish Revival overtones. Domed marble stairs lead to its most impressive room, the Salón de los Espejos (Hall of Mirrors), with interiors by Tiffany of New York. Among the exhaustive displays are fascinating artefacts, such as the tiny suit of astronaut Arnaldo Tamayo (the first Latino in space). Castro's former head of security, Fabian Escalante, claims there have been 638 attempts on the Cuban leader's life, and some comical CIA plots are detailed here, from the exploding cigars to the chemical-infused shoe polish meant to make his beard fall out, thus destroying Castro's power like a modern-day Samson. *Calle Refugio 1, T 861 3858*

15.30 Coppelia

The ice cream at state-run Coppelia is one of few post-revolution luxuries. The vaulted concrete pavilion with irregular coloured glass panels was designed by Mario Girona in 1966. Its spidery arms integrate outdoor courtyards shaded by banyan trees. Locals queue around the block for the day's flavours, and it's an unmissable slice of urban theatre.
Calle 23 y L

17.30 Wall of Flags, Malecón

Dusk brings a city-wide migration towards the seafront for an impromptu party. Join in later, but first witness Cuban-American relations at their most tragi-comic. In January 2006, the US Interests Section set up a giant LED screen in the fifth-floor windows of Harrison & Abramovitz's 1953 embassy building to broadcast scrolling anti-Castro messages, such as *How sad that all the people who know how to run* *this country are driving taxis*. A month later, Castro retaliated by erecting a 138-strong field of 20m-high flagpoles in the car park to obscure the propaganda. This architectural stand-off is completed by the Protestodromo, a vast stage and paved area with ceremonial steel arches built at the height of the Elián González row and used for political rallies, as well as the odd salsa concert (this is Cuba, after all).

21.30 Paladar La Guarida

The restaurant entrance, a curving marble staircase with a Fidel speech and a Cuban flag painted on the peeling plaster wall, is one of the most photographed sites in Havana, especially after La Guarida starred in Tomás Gutiérrez Alea's 1994 film *Fresa y Chocolate*. On the second floor of this former mansion – now a shared-family residence – is the best *paladar* (private restaurant) on the island. Feast on Cuban ceviche, rabbit lasagne or tuna with sugar cane and *yuca a mojo* (cassava, garlic and onions) in a buzzy, multi-roomed space full of curiosities, religious artefacts, antiques and photos of past diners, such as Sean Penn and Benicio del Toro. The quality of service and cuisine comes as a delightful surprise; it's a slick, professional operation. *Concordia 418, T 863 7351, www.laguarida.com*

URBAN LIFE

CAFÉS, RESTAURANTS, BARS AND NIGHTCLUBS

The mojitos and daiquiris are inescapable; the tourist traps are not. So brazenly sip a Havana Club in the art deco of <u>Bar Bacardí</u> (see p065) and open a Castillo de Wajay red in the 1970s lounge at <u>Opus Bar</u> (see p052). Aperitifs are excellent, but Cuba is let down by what comes after. Its contribution to world cuisine, '*a la cubana*', means 'with an egg' and the national dish is *ropa vieja*, literally 'old clothes'. Not inspiring stuff, and perhaps why Castro plonked a Coppelia (see p036) in every city in a 'let them eat ice cream' gesture. However, *paladares* – restaurants run by ordinary Cubans in their own homes, such as La Guarida (see p039) and the daring <u>El Hurzón Azul</u> (Calle Humbolt 153 esq P, T 879 1691) – are steering the city away from *comida criolla* with innovative menus.

Music is everywhere, but make sure to see a world-famous act while in town – salsa from Los Van Van or Paulito FG in <u>Casa de la Música</u> (see p060), *son* from Omara Portuondo in <u>El Delirio</u> (see p068), Silvio Rodríguez's *neuva trova* or reggaeton in <u>Teatro Karl Marx</u> (Avenida 1ra esq 10, T 203 0801), a vast 4,800-capacity venue known simply as Karlos. Cabaret Tropicana (Calle 72, 4505 entre 43 y Línea, T 267 1717) is a cattle market, but Max Borges' concrete telescopic shell vaults, set among tropical foliage, are a triumph of function, location and modernity. You've come for the architecture, not the bum-wiggling and skimpy costumes, right? Right?

For full addresses, see Resources.

Casa de la Amistad

The interiors of the former home of sugar baron Juan Pedro Baró and Catalina Lasa (see p070) are stunning. A paradigm of Cuban eclecticism, the grand, neoclassical exterior resembles an Italian palazzo. But after the 1925 Exposition in Paris, the plans for the rest of the house were changed, and architects Evilio Govantes and Félix Cabarrocas are said to have introduced art deco to the island here in 1927. Lined with Italian and French marble, there are Eygptian references throughout, grillework in *fer forgé* and wall stucco both made in Paris, and sand used for plastering brought from the Nile. Glasswork, such as in the vestibule (above) is by Frenchman René Lalique. Take it all in over dinner at the restaurant Primavera, then listen to live *son* or *boleros* in the garden under the stars. *Avenida Paseo 406 entre 17 y 19, T 831 2823*

El Conejito

Castro was a big fan of The Little Rabbit and would book the 20-seat private room for tête-à-têtes with his private secretary Celia Sanchez. Whether or not the couple went at it like rabbits afterwards is a state secret. The restaurant is hard to miss as it's inexplicably modelled on an English Tudor public house with red brick and dark wood beams. The equally rustic interior resembles a hunting lodge, with its fireplace, ivory bugles and mounted moosehead. The menu would make Glenn Close salivate – not only is rabbit stewed, it's grilled, salted and baked – and with a plentiful supply, this is one establishment which faced no problems during the food shortages. These days it also serves Italian dishes, meat and seafood. After dinner, there's an adjoining karaoke bar – get your own back on the locals with a take on buskers' favourite *Guantanamera*.
Calle M esq 17, T 324 671

A Prado y Neptuno

This project must have looked very good on paper. In a city that had seen little new for decades, architect of the National Art Schools (see p076) Roberto Gottardi was called in to remodel the ground floor of this late 19th-century building into a smart, modern restaurant in 1998. Gottardi got contemporary Emilio Castro (see p090) involved with the interior design, installed Charles Rennie Mackintosh-inspired chairs, pop art-style artwork and, being Italian, hired an Italian chef. But with its green and red colour scheme, *Yanqui*-themed bar and fluorescent lighting, the end result is TGI Fridays circa 1985. Sure, it's buzzy and the comfort-food pizza and pasta are decent, but A Prado y Neptuno makes you worry that this could be the future of Havana. And that's depressing.
Prado y Neptuno, T 860 9636

Café del Oriente

Dining under candelit chandeliers and surrounded by dark wood panelling, heavy drapes, art nouveau floor lamps and a stained glass roof, you could easily be in turn-of-the-century Paris or Vienna. The cuisine is equally European in outlook, with dishes such as chateaubriand with Béarnaise sauce, calf's brains in mustard and brandy cream sauce, the pleasantly rhyming mussels with truffles (try saying that after a few glasses from the extensive wine list) and the best bread on the island. A live trio plays jazz, bossa nova and *son*, and this being a state restaurant, there are five staff per customer. However, unlike other, less refined establishments, it does not take 15 minutes to call their attention; here waiters do the waiting, not you.
Oficios 112 esq Amargura, Plaza de San Francisco de Asis, T 860 6686

El Patio
It's touristy, but the backdrop among the arches of an 18th-century palace is spectacular at night. Bag a table on the balcony overlooking the ornate façade of the 1787 Cuban baroque cathedral, fashioned from black fossilised coral, and order *vaca frita* (fried cow, better than it sounds) with, for the location, *moros y cristianos* (rice and beans).
San Ignacio 54, T 867 1034

Restaurante 1830

The setting of this supperclub complex, in a neoclassical mansion at the mouth of the Rio Almendares, cannot be beaten. Named after the year it was born, interiors are part restored, part eclectic; original iron grilles, late 19th and early 20th century chairs, chandeliers and fireplaces, and art deco-style stained glass in the library, now Bar Colonial, where you should take your aperitif. A red carpet whisks you to an array of dining rooms, with a Cuban and French-influenced menu. The prawns flambéed in rum are delicious, but 1830 can't compete with the culinary magic of Tocororo (T 204 2998) just across the river. However, it's a lot more fun. There is a cabaret (11pm) in the garden and karaoke and a disco on its Japanese-themed island, decorated with stones and shells. Don't ask. *Malecón 1252 esq 20, T 553 091*

Las Ruinas

Architect Joaquín Galvin incorporated the lichen-covered stone walls of a ruined 18th-century sugar mill into his minimalist 1971 design for this Cuban restaurant in Parque Lenin. Branches and creeping tropical flora invade and appropriate the concrete, glass and prefabricated panels, and cantilevered concrete beams overlap trees, blurring the distinction between inside and out. The park itself, 20km outside the city, is a relic of Soviet-Cuban ideals; the provision of space and sports facilities (see p088) for the people came with a catch – Marxist/ Leninist symbolism at every turn. This, combined with the superior cuisine and excellent wine list, meant it was a favourite haunt of Castro, who worked the expense account with foreign diplomats here.
Calle 100 esq Cortina de la Presa, Parque Lenin, T 332 047

Anacaona

This restaurant in Hotel Saratoga (see
p023) takes its name from the all-girl
salsa ensemble who caused a sensation
here when it was the haunt of Havana
high society in the 1930s. After the
revolution, the hotel was appropriated
by Castro, who turned it into a boarding
house for the homeless. Now, after the
hotel reopened in 2005, it's a rare retreat
for foodies as Anacaona boasts one of
the most sophisticated menus in Havana
in an Andalusian/North African themed
setting, with rich fabrics, bell lights, back-
lit latticed wood panels, copper fixtures,
coloured glass mosaics and a cushion-
strewn bar. Treat your palate to snails and
Roquefort followed by sea bass with
rum and saffron, and finish with an *añejo*
(seven-year-old Havana Club rum).
*Hotel Saratoga, Paseo Martí 603 esq
Dragones, T 868 1000,
www.hotel-saratoga.com*

Opus Bar
Come to this 70s lounge bar with your *enamorado* or leave with tears in your eyes after listening to the beautiful, heart-wrenching boleros, sang karaoke-style. With one side all windows and views, the leather armchairs, varnished pine, lace curtains and chipboard ceiling make Opus feel like a step back in time.
4th floor, Teatro Amadeo Roldán, Calle Calzada 512 esq D, T 832 1168

La Casona de 17

Castro's godparents used to live in The Grand House on 17, and you can imagine a bearded toddler playing outside this peach-coloured colonial house, organising his *compadres* into microbrigades. The mansion is separated by folding screens into various dining rooms, some available for hire, contemporary Cuban art hangs on bare yellow walls, there's an impressive art deco stained glass window over the

stairs and exquisite ceiling lights. The kitchen serves up Cuban fare, specialising in *arroz con pollo* cooked in a clay pot (call ahead), paella and meat and seafood grills. Upstairs there's a rare pool table on the terrace looking out at FOCSA (see p010); after dinner, head to its top-floor bar for views and digestifs with the *quinceañeras* and the visiting relatives from Miami. *Calle 17, 60 entre M y N, T 334 529*

El Pedregal

This purpose-built restaurant could only exist in western Havana, where there is space for experimental builds and custom from the conference centre, embassies and science institutes. El Pedregal, which translates as 'the place of stones', was built in the late 1990s and serenely fuses concrete and glass with stone, wood and water, and its terraces overlooking the man-made lake are popular with doting couples. The Cuban and international menu is pretty standard fare but good value and the vintage ports and cognacs are popular with the diplomaterati. After dinner, make the essential pilgrimage to the original Casa de la Música (T 206 6147) in Miramar for some irresistible live salsa.
Calle 23 esq 198, T 273 7831

Gato Tuerto
The One-eyed Cat crouches behind the
National (see p017) in an eclectic Vedado
townhouse remodelled by Evelio Pina in
1960 into a dark, lopsided, intimate venue
for bolero music. Even the garden was
converted into a water feature (there's
no water now, of course). Come to hear
late-night laments by veterans of the
scene, such as Elena Burke and Ela Calvo.
Calle O entre 17 y 19, T 836 0212

La Roca

Just up the road from the Hotel Capri,
in the 1950s playboys and mobsters would
pull into the concrete canopied drive of
this art deco haunt and toss the keys of
their Pontiacs to the valet. That era has
long gone, as has the Capri, but La Roca
remains as solid as... oh, you get the idea.
Turn left as you enter into an intimate,
kaleidoscopic bolthole, which nullifies the
strong Caribbean sun through its randomly
coloured window panes, imitated by the
underlit neon bar. This is one place where
you won't feel guilty about having a midday
snifter; don your Wayfarers and order the
La Roca (white *añejo*, orange and lemon
juice, grenadine and sugar). In contrast,
the restaurant across the hall is cold and
formal, although it hosts regular comedy
nights. One joke not told here, though, is
the old: 'What are the three failures of the
revolution? Breakfast, lunch and dinner.'
Calle 21 y M, T 834 4501

Casa de la Música (Galiano)
This unmissable palace of salsa hosts
wild performances from groups such
as Los Van Van and NG La Banda in the
hulking 1941 art deco América Building,
which was inspired by the Rockefeller
Center. Locals mob the matinees (4-7pm)
featuring Cuban rap and reggaeton; what
all the kids are listening to these days.
*Galiano 267 entre Neptuno y Concordia,
T 860 4165, www.egrem.com.cu*

INSIDER'S GUIDE

ISIS VALDES, MODEL

The fashion industry is in its infancy in Cuba and Isis Valdes is one of few models to have tasted success abroad. However, with many foreign companies now using Havana as a location for photo shoots, agencies have been set up to promote homegrown talent. 'They're grooming the next generation of models at La Maison (see p080),' says Valdes. 'And the shops there are some of the best in Cuba.'

When she's not working, she likes to have a leisurely brunch of tapas in Bodegón Onda (Obrapía esq Baratillo, T 867 1037). 'There's a new delicacy to try every day,' she says. She also recommends Los Nardos (Paseo Martí 563, T 863 2985) for Spanish food. 'There's always a queue and you have to wait for the man at the top of the stairs to call you in,' says Valdes. 'But it's worth it for the paella.' Afterwards she'll visit one of the many museums – a favourite is the Carlos J Finlay Science Museum (Cuba 460, T 863 4824), not least for the views from its roof, which is 'a great place for a mojito'.

For dinner, Valdes loves the idyllic Los XII Apóstoles (Complejo Morro-Cabaña, T 863 8295) or she'll take her friends to the creole restaurant El Aljibe (Avenida 7ma entre 24 y 26, T 204 1583). 'It does the best chicken, rice and beans, and that's saying something in Havana.' Afterwards she'll relax by listening to live music at the Jazz Café (Avenida 1ra esq Paseo, T 553 302). 'It has huge windows right on the Malecón and Havana is so pretty at night.'

For full addresses, see Resources.

ARCHITOUR

A GUIDE TO HAVANA'S ICONIC BUILDINGS

The city's architectural history is almost totally intact as urbanism has been stunted for 40 years. Pre-revolution, huge developments were planned, such as José Luis Sert's gambling and hotel mecca on an artificial island off the Malecón. Instead, economic necessity has preserved outstanding stock that in other cities would have been bulldozed for developers' greed or health and safety rules. Many buildings have simply fallen down, but those that remain, such as the neoclassical villas and ostentatious art deco mansions the upper classes left behind, have been reappropriated. Some were converted to a more socialist function, for example Luis Dediot's decadent Casino Español (Prado y Animas), now the Palacio de los Matrimonios. The rest have been squatted and turned into mixed-family dwellings; houses and later rooms being split and further divided using flimsy screens and improvised mezzanines.

After the revolution, two-thirds of the country's architects left. The idealistic remained and remarkable projects were undertaken, such as the National Art Schools (see p076), until the money and inclination ran dry. Since then, development has been restricted to Soviet-style housing, constructed by microbrigades in suburbs such as Habana del Este. Meanwhile, bright revolutionary imagery has become an inescapable part of the urban fabric: slogans, speeches, mantras and pictures of Che link public and private spaces alike. *For full addresses, see Resources.*

Edificio Bacardí

The rum company left behind a glorious art deco legacy when it fled the country in 1959. Esteban Rodríguez Castell, Rafael Fernández Ruenes and José Menéndez's 1930 tower used Bavarian and Norwegian granite inlaid with brass and embellished with geometrical terracotta reliefs, such as female nudes by Maxfield Parrish and, in a nice Cuban touch, tropical fruit, all topped by the bat emblem. Pass through the lobby to the mezzanine bar to see the exquisite interior (overleaf), with coloured marble, gold leaf, acid-etched glass, blue mirrors, stucco, and mahogany and cedar panels. Connoisseurs should also appreciate the vertical shafts and ziggurats of Edificio López Serrano (Calle 13, 106) by Ricardo Mira and Miguel Rosich, built a year or two later, although it's in a much sorrier state. *Monserrate 261 esq San Juan de Dios*

Lobby, Edificio Bacardí

Teatro Nacional
The curved glass façade of Nicolás Arroyo and Gabriela Menéndez's theatre, built in 1958 and similar to the Royal Festival Hall in London, exposes the lobby and invites the audience in. There's a smaller theatre behind, the two joined by a central tower. See a ballet, or listen to *son* in El Delirio (T 335 713), the club in the protruding fourth floor overlooking the square.
Paseo y 39, Plaza de la Revolución

Cementerio Cristóbal Colón

Havana's cemetery stretches for seven blocks in the centre of town, has its own street grid system and architecture as fascinating as the residential stock, notably the 1933 mausoleum of Catalina Lasa and Juan Pedro Baró (above). French designer René Lalique, who collaborated on the couple's Vedado house (see p041), used Bérgamo marble and onyx to fashion a minimalist white cupola, contrasted by an exquisite door engraved with two reclining angels. As the first woman to get divorced in Latin America in 1918 (to be with Baró), Lasa was buried under 6m of concrete so as not to profane the neighbours. Another must-see is the Borges brothers' concrete, tent-shaped, 1957 Núñez-Gálvez tomb. The cemetery is also the final resting place of musicians Ruben Gonzalez and Ibrahim Ferrer and photographer Alberto Korda.

Edificio Solimar

Among the generally squat architectural hotchpotch and cultural meltdown of Centro rises the seven-storey pink-hued Solimar, now weathered and dulled by its namesakes, the sun and the sea. Radical at the time, Manuel Copado's 1944 poured concrete residential block, which is still in use today, made fine use of an awkward plot, its stretched form maximising levels of light and ventilation, but ultimately the effects of corrosion too. Overlooking the Malecón, its curved, expressive balconies evoke the view of the crashing waves. Around the corner is the alleyway Callejón de Hamel, a colourful, muralled artists' enclave, community project and centre of the Afro-Caribbean religion santería. Join in the Sunday afternoon street carnivals, with live rumba and hypnotic drums.
Soledad 205 esq San Lázaro

Cine La Rampa
This modernist block was converted into a cinema by hydraulically lifting the roof to house the projector. Named in part after its sweeping internal ramp system, which has classic Cuban film posters displayed along its length, it seats 1,000 and houses the national film archive. Don't expect Butterkist or Pepsi, but there is a café and bar, and you can BYO.
La Rampa 111-113 entre O y P, T 878 6146

Cine Yara
The bright convex façade and sloping roof that follows La Rampa's incline have been a Havana fixture since 1947. Junco, Gastón and Domínguez's Radiocentro complex held offices, retail space and TV studios, but these days it's a weekend date venue for 700 teenage couples. Unless it's the Latin American Film Festival (early December), don't venture past the kitschy foyer.
Calle L, 363 esq La Rampa, T 832 9430

Escuelas Nacionales de Arte

Fidel and Che were playing golf at this former country club when they had the idea for an ambitious architectural project: the National Art Schools, to be built on that very spot. Overseen by Ricardo Porro, work began in 1961 in a period of great optimism, reflected in the expressionism of the five buildings: Ballet (left) and Music (above) by Vittorio Garatti, Dramatic Arts by Roberto Gottardi, and Plastic Arts and

Modern Dance by Porro, altogether more sensual ('I made cupolas in the form of breasts,' he said). A concrete shortage was a blessing as the brick Catalonian vaults blended perfectly with the lush setting. As Soviet austerity set in, the schools were abandoned as bourgeois with only three finished; but in 1999 the architects were invited back to complete their masterpiece. *Calle 120, 1110 entre Avenida 9na y 13*

Club Náutico
This overlapping sequence of concrete
shells, designed by Max Borges Recio
in 1953, allows sunlight into a shaded,
airy pavilion. Similar to Borges' earlier
Tropicana (T 267 1717), even down to the
valet canopies, Náutico is less wave-like,
instead resembling giant sea cucumbers.
Post-revolution, it became a club for civil
servants. Slip the guard a *propina* to visit.
Calle 152, Reparto Náutico

SHOPPING

THE BEST RETAIL THERAPY AND WHAT TO BUY

Apart from the perennial must-buys: cigars, rum, music and coffee, Havana used to be a shopping vacuum. But over the last few years, peso shops have been joined by a smattering of touristy boutiques in Habana Vieja. Have a signature scent made at Habana 1791 (Calle Mercaderes 156, T 861 3525), choosing from hundreds of base notes. Treat yourself to the brown stuff at Museo de Chocolate (Calle Mercaderes 255, T 866 4431), where locals flock for Baracoan cocoa bonbons. Casa del Abanico (Obrapía 107, T 863 4452) will hand-paint fans while you wait. Revolutionary art and film posters make good presents (see p086), as do engravings and lithographs at Taller Experimental de Gráfica (Callejón de Chorro 62, T 862 0979). There are lots of galleries where you can buy art too: Centro de Arte Contemporáneo Wifredo Lam (Calle San Ignacio 22, T 861 3419), named after the Cuban surrealist, is one of the best.

Fashion-wise, pick up a loose linen *guayabera* shirt, but don't expect cutting-edge design unless you have a fetish for camouflage or Lycra. However, the constant magazine shoots lured by the city's photogenic backdrop are leaving their mark. La Maison (Avenida 7ma esq 16, T 204 1543), for example, is far more than a 'dollar shop'. Housed in a 1946 villa, it holds a catwalk show by its Aragne Modelling School in the courtyard over dinner at 10pm. It's a fun place to witness the (relatively) monied Miramar social scene. *For full addresses, see Resources.*

La Casona

Contemporary Cuban art is given plenty of space to breathe in this expertly curated gallery set in one of Habana Vieja's most exquisite colonial palaces, the House of the Count of San Juan de Jaruco, which was built in 1737. White-walled exhibition rooms on the first and second floors are set around an inner courtyard; doors are thrown open to allow the strong, natural Caribbean light to flood in from either side. Exhibitions change bi-monthly: past solo shows have featured Jorge López Pardo (above, 'Avistamiento', graphite on linen), Santiago Rodríguez Olazabal and Rigoberto Mena. Nearby on Plaza Vieja is Fototeca de Cuba (T 862 2530), which exhibits the work of Alberto Korda and other revolutionary photographers.
Calle Muralla 107 esq San Ignacio, T 861 8544, www.galeriascubanas.com

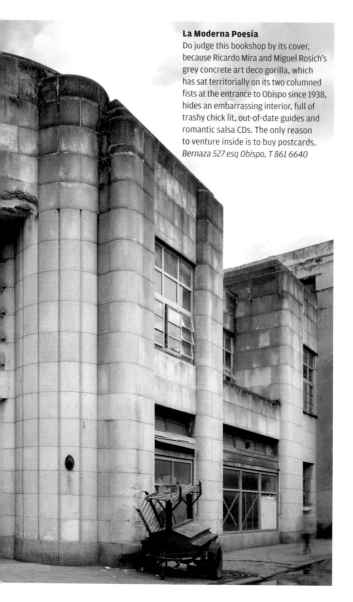

La Moderna Poesía
Do judge this bookshop by its cover, because Ricardo Mira and Miguel Rosich's grey concrete art deco gorilla, which has sat territorially on its two columned fists at the entrance to Obispo since 1938, hides an embarrassing interior, full of trashy chick lit, out-of-date guides and romantic salsa CDs. The only reason to venture inside is to buy postcards.
Bernaza 527 esq Obispo, T 861 6640

La Vajilla

By far your most rewarding buy in this city is genuine period furniture, although the red tape surrounding its exportation can be exhausting and the rules change all the time. South Americans in general are obsessed by the new; Cubans particularly so, due to their lack of exposure to the outside world. Hence the truckloads of antiques and covetables that arrive daily at this two-floored treasure trove, as art nouveau lamps, Cuban mahogany and 19th-century European glassware are unsentimentally thrown out in favour of modern kitsch, reproductions and plastic. La Vajilla is an official shop, so everything has kosher paperwork. Prices seem high until it dawns they're in pesos (£1 = CP50). Bargain, but don't lose focus — you have to get that marble tabletop home somehow.
Avenida Italia 502 esq Zanja, T 862 4751

Farmacia Taquechel

The restoration of not just one but three century-old pharmacies in the old town must be galling for the locals, who clutch prescriptions from some of the best doctors in the world but stare at empty medicine shelves in peso shops. Still, Taquechel is not quite what the doctor ordered, as it sells natural, organic and homeopathic medicines that have been its mainstay since its opening in 1898;

it does a fine line in seaweed cream and shark cartilage should you so desire. Tea tree oil, ylang-ylang, patchouli and lavender are stored in 19th-century French porcelain jars displayed in polished wood cabinets behind the counter with its original till. Out back is a collection of pharmaceutical instruments and books of medicine recipes.
Obispo 155 entre Mercaderes y San Ignacio, T 862 9286

ICAIC

In direct antithesis to Hollywood, post-revolution Cuban silkscreen film posters eschewed individual stars in favour of a minimalist or pop art representation of the *obra* itself. Classic images adorn every inch of the ICAIC foyer (pictured); the posters themselves, plus DVDs of Cuban films, are sold across the road, through the back of the Fresa y Chocolate café.
Calle 23, 1156 entre 10 y 12, T 833 9278

SPORTS AND SPAS
WORK OUT, CHILL OUT OR JUST WATCH

Cuba is a proud sporting nation that punches way above its weight internationally, considering the chronic lack of training facilities. The country won five gold medals in boxing at the 2004 Olympics, while rivalry with the US at baseball is as fanatic and keenly fought as the ideological battle. In a country where daily life is a struggle, state-sponsored sport is, of course, free entertainment, as well as a welcome distraction – like that other great Cuban pastime, sex.

Baseball is played everywhere. Bring your own glove and you could start an innings in a closet, or join in the frenzied support at Estadio Latinoamericano (Zequeria 312, T 706 526). Popular too are basketball and volleyball – catch a game at Sala Kid Chocolate (see p092) or the colourful Estadio Ramón Fonst (Independencia esq Bruzón, T 820 0000). Make a trip to Parque Lenin (Avenida 5ta y 68, T 332 047) for motocross, boating and a swim. For something more sedate, domino wars are waged on foldaway tables in the street. Or make like Fidel and Ernest and charter a boat at Marina Hemingway (Calle 248 esq Avenida 5ta, T 241 150, CUC320 for four hours) and go deep-sea fishing for tuna, blue marlin and wahoo.

Spa culture hasn't reached the island. The best you can hope for is a massage, which might be unusually flirtatious, and a post-lunch dip in a hotel pool – try the Riviera (see p030) for its aquamarine 1950s boards or the Saratoga (see p023) for its Capitolio views. *For full addresses, see Resources.*

Club Habana

Most of the city's members-only beach and sports clubs, such as Max Borges' Náutico (see p078), were handed over to workers' unions after the revolution, but Habana has somehow remained a domain of diplomats and expats. In its previous incarnation as the Havana Yacht Club, this place was so tony that it declined president Batista's membership application because he was *mulato*. These days, it is open to all who pay CUC10 and hand over their papers at the security gate. Carry on up the drive until you see the beaux arts façade of Rafael Goyeneche's 1924 clubhouse. Laze by one of the pools or on the private beach, snorkel in transparent waters, hire a jet ski or find out if anyone's for tennis. If all this exclusivity is making you crave lobster, pad over to one of the two restaurants or BBQ. *Avenida 5ta 188-192, T 204 5700*

Estadio Panamericano
This 35,000-seat, parabolic, Soviet-era stadium by Emilio Castro (no relation) was built in 1989 as a showcase venue for the Panamerican Games in 1991, as was an athletes' village that has become an eastern suburb. The stadium itself is now used only for provincial meets, but at the time, the huge, standard-issue Che mural inspired Cuba to 140 gold medals.
Carretera Vieja de Cojímar, T 814 698

Sala Kid Chocolate

This multi-use indoor sports centre is named after Cuban boxing legend Kid Chocolate (he was small and black; this was long before the days of PC), who was the best fighter in the world in the early 1930s. As well as Friday-night fights, it's used for basketball, judo, badminton, football and handball. Its dilapidated state is masked by a typically colourful Cuban interior and the shafts of sunlight poking through the painted glass and reflecting off the varnish. It's atmospheric, but not the best lighting conditions for top-level sport, although at least the wood floor lends a spring to players' leaps. Four giant murals in the corners display the rewards of perseverance in the face of adversity, such as rain dripping through the roof and regular power cuts. Ask your concierge to find out when one of the national teams is training – watch for just one Cuban peso.

Paseo Martí, opposite Capitolio Nacional

Gimnasio Rafael Trejo

Sandwiched between two blocks in the most depressed, tumbledown corner of colonial Havana, this open-air boxing gym has fostered dreams of greatness (and escape) in eager boys for more than 60 years. It may be raw and primal, like the sport itself, but El Trejo has trained Olympic champions such as Mario Kindelán. Watch the daily training or fights at the weekend.
Calle Cuba 815 entre Merced y Leonor Pérez

ESCAPES

WHERE TO GO IF YOU WANT TO LEAVE TOWN

This chapter has a somewhat insensitive title in a guide to Havana. Many Cubans dream of escape but get no further than the journey between their home and workplace. The transport infrastructure is poor and your mode of travel should be considered carefully. The ex-Russian army planes used for internal flights have a criminal safety record. Cuba has the Caribbean's only rail network, but the chugging stock has been robbed by bandits – on foot. The *especial* tourist train, hilariously dubbed the Orient Express, takes 15 hours to find Santiago. The 1950s Buicks and Chevrolets are photogenic, but a shortage of fuel and parts means they're often off-road. Your best bet is to hail a state-owned, air-con Taxi OK (T 877 6666); the three-and-a-half hour trip to Viñales (see p102) costs CUC45.

Avoid the tourist apartheid at all-inclusive beach resorts such as Varadero, where locals are banned – they're as Cuban as Yorkshire pudding. Instead combine sun worship with a trip to colonial gem Trinidad (see p100) and its *cayos*, or scuba on Isla de la Juventud, where Castro was incarcerated in the 1930s Model Prison, a series of concrete cylindrical structures with rings of cells. Closer to home, bookworms should visit the Museo Ernest Hemingway (Finca Vigía, T 910 809), while the Las Terrazas UNESCO biosphere reserve is a 1960s eco-village, whose organic restaurant El Romero (T 204 3739, www.lasterrazas.cu) does incredible things with chickpeas.

For full addresses, see Resources.

Cienfuegos

It can be a struggle to meet real Cubans in Havana, as *jinteros* (literally 'jockeys', looking to take you for a ride) shadow your every move. Get out of the capital to experience the warmth and generosity of the people in one of the provincial towns. Leafy, lazy Cienfuegos was founded by Frenchman Louis de Clouet in 1819, and the neoclassical architecture and wide boulevards demonstrate how the French differed from the Spanish in their approach to colonial urban planning. Built by the cane, Cienfuegos' boom years were 1890 to 1930 and the stand-out address is the 1917 Palacio de Valle (Calle 37, 3501). Sugar baron Acisclo del Valle brought craftsmen from Morocco to work on his neo-Moorish indulgence, an architectural boast of his fortune. He later went bankrupt. Drown his sorrows with a rum on the roof terrace.

Boca de Guamá
This ecotouristy centre is Cuba's answer to the Everglades, a huge expanse of swamp, forest and freshwater lagoons (perfect for scuba diving) home to 115 endemic plant species, 160 types of bird and Rhombifier and Acutus crocodiles. Turn the tables with a croc steak lunch on your way to Cienfuegos (see p097).
Gran Parque Natural Montemar,
Peninsula de Zapata, T 04 593 224

Trinidad

This UNESCO World Heritage Site founded in 1514 on Cuba's south coast was a sleepy hamlet until the 19th century, when riches from the sugar trade began to flood in. At one stage, the city's surrounding Valle de los Ingenios was producing a third of the island's crop from 70 mills. Sugar barons, merchants and slave-trade plantation owners turned Trinidad into the colonial jewel it is today, with its grandiose palaces and mansions, cobblestones, stained glass and red-tiled roofs, overseen by the bell tower (above) of the former San Francisco de Asís convent. Trinidad is six hours from Havana, so stay awhile. Spend your days on paradise island Cayo Blanco de Casilda, scuba diving at its black coral reef among turtles, and nights at The Cave, dancing among the stalactites in a beautifully lit cavern. Just watch out for the bats.

Playas del Este

Havana's closest beaches are 20km to the east and city folk flock here on weekends. It's not exactly a tropical paradise, but if you can ignore the odd oil rig, it's a more authentic experience than at many of the island's sanitised resorts. However, it's not just sun and salsa that should bring you to this 10km stretch between Bacuranao and Guanabo – after the 1958 tunnel under the harbour opened up Habana del Este as a viable suburb, urban development here was initially influenced by the satellite city concept in Europe. The 1970s and 1980s saw the birth of the community housing projects of the microbrigades, and latterly came Villa Panamericana (see p090). Top up your tan at party central Santa Maria del Mar or the more sedate (read ex-pat) Club Mégano, which has sparklingly clear water, catamarans, windsurfing and jet skis.

Valle de Viñales

This lush, verdant, limestone landscape 160km to the south-west of Havana is punctuated by table-top mountains and underground caverns, and has a climate that's perfect for growing tobacco. The plantations here supply many of the cigar factories in Havana, including Partagás (see p034), and the conditions give rise to the earthy, dense, rich-bodied taste of its own-brand *puros*. In the pretty village of Viñales itself, the pace of life is slower than in Havana, but the partying lasts just as long. Accommodation mainly caters for backpackers in myriad *casas particulares*. You should chill by the pool in Hotel Los Jazmines (T 08 796 205), out of town on a hill overlooking the valley. From Viñales, continue to Maria La Gorda, at the far western tip of the island, for some of the best scuba diving in the Caribbean.

NOTES

SKETCHES AND MEMOS

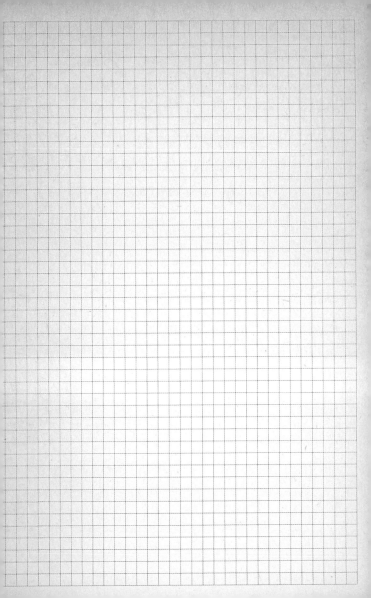

RESOURCES
CITY GUIDE DIRECTORY

A

El Aljibe 062
Avenida 7ma entre 24 y 26
T 204 1583

Anacaona 050
Hotel Saratoga
Paseo Martí 603 esq Dragones
T 868 1000
www.hotel-saratoga.com

B

Bar Bacardí 040
Edificio Bacardí
Monserrate 261 esq San Juan de Dios

Boca de Guamá 098
Gran Parque Natural Montemar
Peninsula de Zapata
T 04 593 224

Bodegón Onda 062
Obrapía esq Baratillo
T 867 1037

C

Cabaret Tropicana 040
Calle 72, 4505 entre 43 y Línea
T 267 1717

Café del Oriente 045
Calle Oficios 112 esq Amargura
Plaza de San Francisco de Asis
T 860 6686

Capitolio Nacional 009
Calle Industria y Barcelona
T 860 3411

Carlos J Finlay
Science Museum 062
Calle Cuba 460 entre Amargura y Brasil
T 863 4824

Casa del Abanico 080
Obrapía 107
T 863 4452

Casa de la Amistad 041
Avenida Paseo 406 entre 17 y 19
T 831 2823

Casa de la Música (Galiano) 060
Galiano 267 entre Neptuno y Concordia
T 860 4165
www.egrem.com.cu

Casa de la Música (Miramar) 055
Calle 20 esq 35
T 206 6147

La Casona 081
Centro de Arte La Casona
Calle Muralla 107 esq San Ignacio
T 861 8544
www.galeriascubanas.com

La Casona de 17 054
Calle 17, 60 entre M y N
T 334 529

Centro de Arte Contemporáneo
Wifredo Lam 080
Calle San Ignacio 22 esq Empedrado
T 861 3419

Cine La Rampa 072
La Rampa 111-113 entre O y P
T 878 6146

Cine Yara 074
Calle L 363 esq La Rampa
T 832 9430

Club Náutico 078
Calle 152
Reparto Náutico

El Conejito 042
Calle M esq 17
T 324 671

Club Habana 089
Avenida 5ta 188-192
T 204 5700

HOTELS
ADDRESSES AND ROOM RATES

Casa Raul 016
  Room rates:
  Two-bedroom villa, CUC350
  Calle 15, 153 entre 6 y 8
  T 290 1491
  www.cubaccommodation.com

Hotel Florida 022
  Room rates:
  double, CUC160;
  Suite 18, CUC200
  Obispo 252 esq Cuba
  T 862 4127
  www.habaguanex.com

Hotel Los Jazmines 102
  Room rates:
  double, CUC55
  Carretera de Viñales
  Valle de Viñales
  T 08 796 205

Hotel Nacional de Cuba 017
  Room rates:
  double, CUC 170;
  Suite Especial, CUC400;
  Real, CUC600;
  Presidential, CUC1000
  Calle O esq 21
  T 836 3564
  www.hotelnacionaldecuba.com

Hotel Raquel 028
  Room rates:
  double, CUC180-CUC200;
  Junior Suite, CUC230-CUC250
  Calle Amargura esq San Ignacio
  T 860 8280
  www.habaguanex.com

Hotel Santa Isabel 016
  Room rates:
  double, CUC240
  Calle Baratillo 9 entre Obispo y Narciso
  López Plaza de Armas
  T 860 8201
  www.habanaguex.com

Hotel Riviera 030
  Room rates:
  double, CUC130
  Paseo y Malecón
  T 836 4051
  www.grancaribe.cu

Hotel Saratoga 023
  Room rates:
  Junior Suite Saratoga,
  CUC280-CUC330;
  Suite Habana, CUC650-CUC670
  Paseo Martí 603 esq Dragones
  T 868 1000
  www.hotel-saratoga.com

La Mansion 016
  Six-bedroom villa, CUC2000
  T 205 7959
  www.rentincuba.com

Meliá Cohiba 020
  Room rates:
  double, CUC170
  Avenida Paseo entre 1ra y 3ra
  T 833 3636
  www.solmeliacuba.com

Palacio Cueto 016
  Room rates:
  price on request
  Calle Inquisidor 351 esq Mercaderes
  www.habaguanex.com

Sofitel Sevilla Hotel 033
Room rates:
double, CUC206;
Double Superior, CUC260
Calle Trocadero 55 entre Zulueta
y Avenida de los Misiones
T 860 8560
www.sofitel.com
Tryp Habana Libre 026
Room rates:
Standard Double, CUC200;
Double Vista Panorámica, CUC220;
Junior Suite, CUC300;
Suite 'Governor', CUC660
Calle L esq 23
T 834 6100
www.solmeliacuba.com

WALLPAPER* CITY GUIDES

Editorial Director
Richard Cook

Art Director
Loran Stosskopf
City Editor
Jeremy Case
Project Editor
Rachael Moloney
Executive
Managing Editor
Jessica Firmin
Travel Bookings Editor
Sara Henrichs

Chief Designer
Ben Blossom
Designer
Ingvild Sandal

Map Illustrator
Russell Bell

Photography Editor
Christopher Lands
Photography Assistant
Jasmine Labeau

Chief Sub-Editor
Jeremy Case
Assistant Sub-Editor
Milly Nolan

Wallpaper* Group
Editor-in-Chief
Jeremy Langmead
Creative Director
Tony Chambers
Publishing Director
Fiona Dent

Contributors
Paul Barnes
Jeroen Bergmans
Alan Fletcher
David McKendrick
Claudia Perin
Meirion Pritchard
Ellie Stathaki
Maria Aseneth Yepes

PHAIDON

Phaidon Press Limited
Regent's Wharf
All Saints Street
London N1 9PA

Phaidon Press Inc
180 Varick Street
New York, NY 10014
www.phaidon.com

First published 2007
© 2007 Phaidon
Press Limited

ISBN 978 0 7148 4722 1

A CIP Catalogue record
for this book is available
from the British Library.

All prices are correct at
time of going to press,
but are subject to change.

Printed in China

PHOTOGRAPHERS

HAVANA
A COLOUR-CODED GUIDE TO THE HOT 'HOODS

PLAZA DE LA REVOLUCIÓN
One million Cubans regularly squeeze into this symbolic square for a Castro monologue

MIRAMAR
Boulevards are lined with mansions housing embassies, dollar shops and restaurants

HABANA VIEJA
The colonial core has more than 4,000 listed buildings, from baroque to art nouveau

LA RAMPA
This street is a non-stop strip of classic hotels and cinemas, fast-food joints and nightclubs

EL VEDADO
Neoclassical villas and art deco towers flank theatres, cultural centres and leafy parks

PARQUE CENTRAL
Horses and carriages await outside hotels and museums in this touristy main square

For a full description of each neighbourhood,
including the places you really must not miss, see the Introduction